grief & loss & love & sex

PREFACE

Some time around 2001 or so, I was walking down the street in Cabbagetown (Toronto) and when I stopped at a corner near Allen Gardens to wait for the light to turn, a man, who may have lived in the park, appeared beside me and caught my eye. I remember how he seemed to look right into my soul, and he said to me, "*Never stop doing what you're doing.*" Bewildered, I said, "*What do you mean?*" He said, "*Never stop writing poetry.*" When I turned back around he'd vanished, like an apparition. But the essence of him has stayed with me always. I couldn't identify him if my life depended on it. But, I have carried him with me. And, he has continued to both encourage and mystify me for nearly two decades.

Who was he? How did he know? Nobody knew but me.

I did stop for a while. Many times. I always came back to it again, but I never found the courage to share it with the world. I suppose I'd allowed myself to believe those who'd told me to be a writer was an unrealistic and unworthy pursuit. *Respectable* people. People who didn't live in the park. I'd allowed them to get under my skin, integrated their narrow beliefs as my own.

When my eldest sister died by suicide something inside me cracked open. The words began to trickle out as I sat oceanside in Eleuthera searching for her in the sunrise, then came in a steady stream with increasing urgency. My heart was broken and I needed to mend it. There was a tear in the Universe and I needed a way to stitch it together again. There were missing pieces of me I suddenly urgently needed to find. And, I did.

Here is a collection of poems written and compiled in the weeks immediately following her death. They have been my healers.

I hope you will find something of value to you within them.

grief & loss & love & sex

lara margaret marjerrison

"Even when your voice is shaking, you still have a voice."

my friend Cee

TABLE OF CONTENTS

INTRODUCTION

I'd put my phone on airplane mode before bed that night. I was weary from the afternoon's memorial for a friend who had OD'd on New Year's Eve and wanted to sleep undisturbed.

Also, woo-woo as this might sound, I had spoken to a psychic or medium or clairvoyant--I can't recall the specific term she uses--just the morning before and, without me having told her a single detail about myself or my family, she relayed to me that she was receiving an urgent message of "*sister, sister, sister, sister, sister.. and something about the number twenty-eight.*" She went on to say that my sister was "*...tired of being the matriarch in the family. She wanted an intervention, wanted my mother, my other sister, and me to do something...to help her.*" I had spent two entire days ruminating on a) how to tell my mother and sister I was getting advice from psychics without them thinking I was whacko and b) how to stage an intervention for a woman who already knew everything, was always right, and was in no way predisposed to taking advice, least of all from her baby sister.

I was weary from all that thinking too. I was desperate to come up with a solution and was coming up with nothing. My little inside voice had been nagging me all day to call her. I knew she'd had a tough week and in the weeks leading up to that one I had been making every effort to be there for her, stay in constant contact, offer her some kind of hope to hang onto. But, that night I just didn't have the energy for the conversation. I promised myself I would call her in the morning.

I woke up to a text message sent twice from my brother-in-law, Stuart, urging me to call him. Stuart never sends text messages. Not to me anyway. He's married to my middle sister, Susan, who has a heart condition, and when I called and heard the strain in his voice my mind immediately jumped to its worst conclusion-- that she had had a heart attack. He choked on his words when he told me she was okay.. it was my other sister. It was Catherine. His voice trailed off as he couldn't bring himself to say out loud what had actually happened.

But, I knew.

Catherine had told me in advance of her plans. On her birthday in fact, October 17, 2017. She explained how she had a list of reasons to live and a list of reasons to die and the *to-die* list was longer and, unless that changed, she intended to follow through. She had been increasingly immobilized and in pain for four years following a cycling accident and she was losing all sense of hope for recovery. The idea of life without movement was intolerable to her. She had chosen an end-date of November thirtieth. Things needed to be better by then.

I told her how I remembered that feeling of hopelessness vividly, the moment just before my own attempted suicide in 1998 when I surrendered to it. I didn't want her to do it and I hoped she'd change her mind, but I understood if she was intent on it there was little I could do to stop her. I asked only that she let me say goodbye. That day she promised me she would.

When we surpassed her date, I allowed myself to believe she wouldn't do it. On January twenty-eighth, she did.

Twenty-eight. Turns out that psychic was onto something.

My sister broke her promise. I didn't get to say goodbye. Nobody did.

In the aftermath, I found myself needing a place to go to try to reconcile the irreconcilable. I knew I needed the ocean and the jungle and to be away from people. I wanted serenity and solitude. I didn't have any idea where I would find such a place, so I asked the Universe to show me. Okay.. so I'm a bit woo-

woo. Almost immediately after I put that request out to the ether, I distractedly logged onto Instagram (as one does) and the first thing that popped up in my feed was a post from Lenny Kravitz tagged on the island of Eleuthera. Now, for years and years I have referred to myself as an "Eleutheromaniac"--kind of a made-up word, I think--meaning *one possessing an irresistible desire for freedom*. Freedom is my number one. But I had no idea a PLACE called Eleuthera, a PLACE called Freedom (which is what the word means in Greek) existed. Yet.. there it was. And, so it was that one tiny act by one bonafide rock star, sharing his world from two-thousand miles away, became the perfect answer to my prayer. Little did he know. I booked a flight, packed a bag, and left to sit by the ocean and stare into the sunrise and search for answers in the sand. And, as I sat there the words began to flow. And, they didn't stop for six straight months. And, they became *grief & loss & love & sex*.

So, here we are.

One of my main observations as I've moved through this grief is this: yes.. ultimately our journey is singular. Each of us gets to choose how we live and how we die, whether we believe it's within our control or not. As with life, our death will be the consequence of a choice or series of choices we've made. Life basically comes down to just that: choices followed by consequences which lead to choices that lead to consequences, and so on. But, here's what's also true: our choices have impact on more than just us. Just as Lenny's choice to share a simple moment of beauty on Instagram became an answer to my prayer, my sister's choice became my and my family's nightmare. I think too often we forget our contribution to cause and effect. We are part of something greater than our individual selves, whatever you may want to call it.

Many of us have been affected by suicide, either because we've lost someone, or many someones, or because we've spent nights awake contemplating our own. I acknowledge its presence, its prevalence, and its allure. I hope in this moment **you** are okay and, if you're not, you'll speak to someone and let them know, mindful of the laws of cause and effect. I say this without judgment or any attempt at shaming you. I say it because I care about you as a human being (for real) and because I know that, for someone who loves you, to lose you would be unbearable, contrary to what the demons might be whispering in your ear even as you read these words. I say it from direct personal experience, from my intimate understanding of both sides of the conversation. There *IS* light on the other side of that all-consuming darkness.

What this book is intended to do is to reveal to you some of my own process of coming to terms with the impact of suicide and healing from a pain that ripped through me with the force of a tsunami, leaving me forever changed.

In wholly giving myself over to grief and loss and love and sex, I found that my rawest human emotions became tangled, so intimately intertwined that it has become difficult at times to distinguish one from another. There is agonizing sadness. There is anguish and anger. There is compassion and understanding. There is shock and disbelief. Still. There is longing and desire and loneliness. There is laughter returning. There is acceptance, somewhere just out of reach, but slowly taking form. There is more than all of that combined, some of it too in-my-face to eloquently articulate, some I'm only just discovering, peeling back the layers of. Some beautiful. Some horrific. Some tragic. All of it occurring at once

Inside the pages of *grief & loss & love & sex* we'll move through a few of those pieces together and see where we end up.

grief & loss & love & sex

do something that makes you breathe

my sister's advice

proof of my existence
is not conditional
upon your acknowledgment of me
i am here
whether you see me
or not

i.am.elemem

she noticed
she didn't like the feeling
of needing other people

loner

april twenty-eight
two zero one eight

three months today
still feels like yesterday
suspended animation
continued sublimation
time hanging on a hook
places i can't look

away

moving in and out of opposites
deconstructing, reconstructing
life and death as composites
resurrecting old emotions
so i can let them go
marinating in the question of
to know or not to know

how

now i'm living in a paradox
you, you were living in an airtight box
mirages in your mind
stealing from you over time

ensnared like a prisoner
in a tale that wasn't true
visions of your own demise
so powerful they took you
far away, beyond the sunrise
to a place that we can't go

where

opiate of the masses
dissolved in the water in the glass
on the table by the bed
beside the letter where you said how
ours was a constant stream of joys and sorrows
i'm sorry to miss the rest of your tomorrows
i hope you'll remember me in good times more than bad
i hope my voice in your head will still be comfort
when you're sad
i love you

cath

a lemon yellow Lady Macbeth
her smile fills a room
while she thinks about death
and seeks out a soul to consume
in the room
a lemon yellow chair sitting there
and in it hides a lock of his hair
and the lady ponders on about death
in the gloom
of the evening
there's the sound of her breath
and she fears not this thing they call death
and she won't be beholden to doom
and she basks in the light of the moon
in her town
where the crazy circus world spins around
in her head
where the candyman tells her that she's already dead
where the fat lady sings
and the supper bell rings
where lions and tigers and grotesquely pretty things
live for the spotlight
and the warmth that it brings
and the lock of his hair
is still hiding there
in a lemon yellow chair
for Macbeth

circus world

the sky came down
to touch the ground
and grant me another try
to say goodbye
i don't know how i did
don't know if it transmitted
but for a little while
i felt you there
reassuring me
with your gentle touch
just like you did
when i was a kid
when you soothed away
my fears and tears
looked after me
for all those years
so many chances
to properly thank you
i let slip away
but, underneath
this sky today
with you on your way
to someplace i can't reach
in my heart and on my skin
i felt you once more
take me in
when i allowed
surrender to begin
someplace within
still.. i want you back
i wanted you to stay
i just can't believe
it has to end this way

goodbye

forty-five years old
with a stack of dead friends
i wonder
if i laid them end to end
could i build a bridge
o'er this chasm of despair
that threatens to swallow us all

how small
do i feel
when i realize it's real
how powerless to conceal
how desperately i feel i must stop it
God, how i wish i could stop it

gun violence
radio silence
mass shootings
department store lootings
suicide bombs amidst the throngs
and, a stabbing mistaken
for performance art

wherefore art our sensibilities
is there still such a thing as humanity
humility

ADHD and ADD, PCP and DDT, OCD and PTSD
the world is too harsh
for the fragile people
if suicide doesn't get you
cancer will
whatever your poison
in a world full of poison
poison kills

it eats you from the inside out
it eats me from the inside out
we all want out

poison

the shock wore off
and the pain set in
and i searched around
for a place to begin
again

restart

if you're looking for God
out there somewhere
in the ether
or hanging from
a symbol of some kind
you're looking in the wrong direction
it's within
you're it
that's what terrifies you
the power has been inside you all along

finding god

grief
all waxing and waning
as moody as the moon
swooning in to the dark of my room
with her, *hey.. you up*
can we just sit up and stare a while
at the clock beside the bed
replay just one more time
all the memories
in your head
remember every bit of every bit
that ever was
and now will never be
she torments me
boasting of her power
to bring me to my knees
then ghosting
and leaving me in a heap
of beginning again
i squeeze my eyes shut
to block her from view
so i can steal just a few
more precious hours of rest
head under the pillow
legs curled to my chest
like a child who's been shaken
when i awaken
i stagger to the table
where i sit
to make art
(hand-painted protection)
to keep her from taking
the whole of my heart
with her when she goes
pieces of it still remain
though not the same

i'm filling in the cracks with gold
so it doesn't appear
so battered and old
Kintsugi
the art of precious scars
and as i sit i wonder
do you now walk among the stars

kintsugi

i need to get out
(of my head) more

a-ha moments

i found myself
in a place called freedom
on the edge of a cliff
overlooking the sea
while the waves
rolled in and receded
the shore received them
and the ocean
welcomed them back again
leaving me still
in a place called freedom

eleuthera

there's a blank space inside my mind
a nothingness i can't define
an ocean of space you used to fill
a place i go and search for you still
but, you're not there
and, i can't find you anywhere

an eerie calm in an answerless abyss
the island gives me gifts like this
the ocean tides pull the tears from my eyes
when i speak to you through every sunrise
longing for resolution i can't yet feel
nothingness becomes me, everything's surreal

i don't know how to thank you
don't know how to say goodbye
don't know how to say i'm sorry
for all the years we let slip by

i don't know how to reconcile the way
your life fell into dust
i keep thinking you're still here
can't seem to adjust
to the hole you left behind
like a chasm in my chest
did you find the peace you sought
have you laid yourself to rest

trying to find the words to speak my pain
makes me feel it all, all over again
i re-live that phone call
and the way you used to say my name
you live on inside me
but nothing is the same

i understand your reasons
know you felt justified
and in my heart of hearts
can even empathize
but hate the way you put a pain you couldn't bear
into our mother's eyes

now we carry your remains
in tiny vials 'round our necks
and i sit here by this ocean
seeking ways i can collect
a thousand memories to cling tight to
with the final words you said that day..
it'll be okay, Lar. it'll be okay

abyss

you think you can hold me
under your thumb
reign me in
contain me
blame me
for forty-plus years
of history
as if every error of ways made
was my responsibility
i was a kid
and now i'm a woman
wild as the wolves
who run free
i am my own, and only my own
i answer only to me
no man man-handles me
you cannot tame me
claim me
as your own personal circus monkey
trained to behave
the way you want me to be

i will not be vilified for my existence
crucified for my opinions
denied my liberty
chained by some story
you've made up in your head
and chosen to believe
about all the ways i've done wrong
don't belong
in the world into which i was born
if you surmise otherwise
you've not been paying attention
step out of my way, son
yea, though i walk through the valley
of the shadow of death
i will walk free
'til my last breath

wild as the wolves

it's a dangerous thing
to elevate a man
to such a height
as to become incapable
of listening critically
to the words he speaks
rather clinging to each one
as though it's a pearl

deification

if you truly wish to understand me
you must open to the possibility
that you have misunderstood
everything about me
before now

see through

i'd built myself
a cage
in the shape of my desires
it was up to me
to set me free

traps we fall into

time after time
sign after sign
the universe showed me
that you were the one
you showed me
something different
with your duck and run
i was forced to take
your word over hers

actions speak louder

in one single
heart-shattering moment
of despair
i reached out to you
but you weren't there
all you sent back
was radio silence
the subtlest form of violence
against a woman
and it sunk into my belly
like a brick
you're just not equipped
to meet me there
where humanity meets humility
set aside your self
to care for me
in a moment of need
a moment of truth
there was the proof
so just like that
i dropped you
stepped over the remains
of the day
and carried on my way
as though
i'd never picked you up
to begin with

i mean, really
let's be straight
who needs the extra weight

sayonara

you stand and reflect
while i project my desires
unrequited love

haiku

you appeared solid
you turned out to be
just fluff

illusions

every night
i dream of you
in erotica
and romance
and tender loving sin
tell me
how the hell i carve you
out from under my skin

out, damned spot!

should i ask how it is
i found you here
in this, the strangest of places
or shall i steer clear
of that topic for the time being
the one of you
wearing more than one
of your faces
the one where you're living a dream
that isn't your dream
where inside
you're living
somewhere in between
where your body moves one way
your mind another
your heart can't determine
if one way's the other
so you stay
despite knowing you don't really belong
and you stray
when the pull of your heart is stronger
than knowing it's wrong
is it wrong

i see you

there are times i turn myself
completely inside out and expose
the most vulnerable pieces
i marvel at my compulsion toward
such masochistic tendencies
what makes me want to
show you my underbelly
i might as well
hand you a scalpel
and show you where to cut

senses & sensibilities

icons in her eyes
social mediocrity
swallowing her life

haiku 2

i don't care
what degrees you have
what your address is
how much money is in your bank account
i don't care how many Facebook friends
you have or how many likes
you got on Instagram yesterday
i want to know what you've endured
what you're willing to give up
for what, or whom, you love
what you're willing to suffer for
i want to know not
what you would spend a million on
but what you would do with your last dollar
i want to know what breaks your heart
and i want to know
what makes it soar
i want to hear the stories you tell yourself
in the dark of night
when no one else is listening
i want to know
who are you then

when you're alone

how do you measure your worth
did you not bring it with you at birth
isn't your mere existence enough
proof that you are worthy of love
do you need *more* than self-love to define
yourself as Divine
do you rely on some external source
to validate every course of action
you ever undertake
how much sense does that make
you came here knowing
as wise as any sage bestowing
gems of erudition upon disciples
you could write your own bible
it is the story of your life
a story of serenity and strife
of mirth and sometimes misery
but, ultimately a victory
in that you are still here standing tall
despite many and varied forces vying to make you feel small
you need nothing outside yourself
put those ideas up high upon a shelf
and leave them there to rot
while you get on with what you've got
which is nothing less than the whole of the multiverse
at your disposal, not the converse
later go back and retrieve them
and to be sure you don't once more begin to believe them
use them as compost to enrich
the soil of the garden in which
you will plant your own Eden
let your detractors call you a heathen
they only grasp at something to believe in
clinging to their shields
fearing slings and arrows in the words you wield
when you speak your own mind

might penetrate the ties that bind
them to their holy houses of cards
and force them to acknowledge the shards
of truth in what you say
it's uncomfortable that way
forgive them for they know not what they do
know not that they too
are the Universe personified
begotten from stardust
on a journey of ten million years
let that knowledge quell your fears
then lift your face to the sun, my precious flower
inside your own heart lies all the power

measure for measure

i wish you
more laughter than tears
more excitement than fears
more joy than sorrow
a richer tomorrow
i wish you
bliss and blessings
from below and above
most of all
i wish you love

wishes

i want to hold
my hand up to yours
read your story
through the whorls
of my eager fingertips
explore every piece
of you that exists
kiss every experience
from your lips
taste every place you've ever been
breathe every sight you've ever seen
live a thousand sensate dreams
bask in energetic beams
radiating from each pore in your skin
listen to the waves
from the place they begin
inside the ocean
of your soul
relinquish every ounce of control
trade it all in
for the whole
of just being
with you

gestalt

something in your eyes
something tantalizing
something i can't name
that makes you and me the same
levelled me up when i was low
guided me when i didn't know
which direction i was meant to go
forgot my *as above, so below*

you brought me to a place i now call home
reminded me i'm never alone
raised my vibration
dissolved my alienation
swept away my isolation
inspired the creation
that poured out of my heart
every pregnant moment, living art

your voice in my ear
your song on my lips
your smile in my eyes
my heart doing flips then
settling into your groove where it fits
like a glove
on the hand of God
manifested in my very fingertips
reaching out to touch your face
inviting you in to my sacred space

i've been many places
looked into many faces
been around the world and back
found nothing that i lack
but a love so pure and sacred
it allows me to stand naked
before you without guilt or shame
like Magdalene with Yeshua, we're the same
baby, we're the same

let's love like that again
show the world
a love like that again
call me, baby
call my name
i'm Magdalene

call my name (dear god)

endings
that are also beginnings
losses
that morph into winnings
the great paradoxical theory of change
the more i let go
the more i retain
the less i am sure
the more that remains
to be found
in the steady
rhythm of my
beating heart
it matters not
that we're worlds apart
that only means we have more room
to tend to this place
where the flowers bloom
where the sunshine finds us
and the stars alight
when you whisper in my ear at night
and tell me all will be alright
and laughter finds my throat again
when i allow sadness to move through
and life's promise
that all shall be renewed
proves true
for even in death
i found you

i found you

i lost my mind and came to my senses
when i met you
surrendered my heart, dropped my defences
when one became two

the scent of a woman
the touch of a man
the way my skin quivers
at the touch of your hand

how my body aches for you
arches back and waits for you
takes you in and quakes for you
there is no other place for you
but here

come inside

when you press the tip
of your wand
to my lips
and whisper incantations
of love
as ancient as the Dead Sea scrolls
the way the words roll
off your tongue, every one
a psalm, like a balm
for a broken soul
your magic courses through me
brings me to my knees
that chafe and bleed
from the hours spent there
in prayer, before you
prone and weeping
the waters of life
seeping through
every question ever formed
in the bases of our minds
slips into an abyss
of bliss
when we surrender
to the truth
of what is happening
in this moment
and you open me up
like a good book
and find that place
that only you can reach
each and every
nerve ending
exposed
like tendrils in the garden
heart and mind transposed
with Heaven and Earth

i can feel the way you want me
to scream out His name
in vain and ecstasy
for the moment
that came just before
the splitting of two souls
into one
we have begun
our ascent into higher realms

this is the way
the truth
the life

make me your wife

answered prayers

what if i reached out to touch you
what if you reached back to me
what if i pulled you in closer
what if you didn't resist
what if we kissed
what if a breeze was blowing
what if we danced in the mist
what if we kissed
what if your arm slipped around me
what if you loved how it felt
what if in my eyes you noticed
all your reservations melt
what if i walked around you
slowly in circles
tracing my fingers over your skin
what if we could no longer distinguish
where i end and you begin
what if the world stopped spinning
what if we just stood still
what if what each of us was seeking
was the very thing the other could fulfill
how fiercely you guard your freedom
i understand
i do that too
we inhabit the edges of this world
while longing to touch the sky
your fear warns you
you might get smothered
but, dear one
what if i'm the very one
who came to teach you how to fly

come fly with me

it is, at times, critical
to look at
your current set
of circumstances
with a completely fresh
set of eyes
in this way
gratitude and wonder
will remain
at the forefront

look again

like the whisper of a butterfly wing
the slightest flutter on a distant shore
one tiny gesture made by you
touched down on me like a gentle kiss
two thousand miles away or more
transporting you through space and time
to come knocking down my door
to wake up angels who'd been sleeping
in the cracks of my fractured heart
to give them back their voices
remind them every moment fully lived
is a living work of art

you continued on unaware
of the effect you'd had on me
oblivious to the way your spark became my flame
never knowing what a difference your existence made
to a stranger—you don't even know my name
but i stand before you here and now
as proof of our existence intertwined
demonstrating how your very heartbeat affects mine
never mind the distance in space or time
like everything we claim to know
those too are mere illusions
we are waveforms rippling outward
we are spirits playing human

we should never compromise our selves
to try to placate one another
never trade in our integrity
for a chance to prove our worth
never bend to others' judgements
about who we're meant to be
never let external voices
steal what is ours by birth
but we must remember in each moment
those forces ever at play
every choice in every moment
every action every moment every day
ripples outward through the waves
of light and sound and thought
leaving imprints on the world around us
whether we're aware or not

see.. we belong to one another
so let's hold on to one another
act from kindness and from love
choose to rise above
so that every ripple outward
leaves an imprint on a heart
like the one you left on mine
when you turned it into art

the butterfly effect

forget not
to find
the beauty of the world
seek it, in fact
though your duty it may be
to take up arms
against injustices
be motivated by love
not hatred
for hatred will cause
your heart
to shrivel and go cold
you will forget
the reasons
for which you fight
and the world
will be left colder still
more barren and devoid
of the beauty
for which you sought justice
to begin with

let love rule

when you spoke of others
i took a moment to remind you
there are no others
there is no us and them
there is only we
there is no separation
between us and them
you and me
we are one
and the time has come
to free our hands of weapons
to choose instead to step in
to the soil of our minds
and plant the seeds of change
from which a different world can grow
listen to the sound of your heart
like the rain beating down
on fertile ground
it knows
it knows
it knows
what we reap
so shall we sow

there are no others

i capture my thoughts
like butterflies
in a net
then pin them to a page
for conservation
objects for observation
set into form
no longer weightless
and free
if i share them with you
will you carry them back
into the wild
for me

catch and release

A FEW WORDS FROM MY SISTER

The last piece of advice my sister ever gave me was, "*Go do something that makes you breathe.*"

I had been reorganized out of a job just three weeks before she died and the first thing I did was call her. Because that's what you did when there was a crisis to be managed. You called Catherine. She was the fixer. Her advice to me, after patiently allowing me to vent my emotion and frustration, was, "*Go right now and do something that makes you breathe--swim, walk, anything. Your breath will make it better. You'll be able to respond from a better place then.*" And, suddenly (ludicrously late in life) I understood the benefit of fitness (her passion) in a way I hadn't before. It has nothing to do with a perfect body or perfect score (though, let's be honest, she DID love to win). It's about moving breath through. It's about life force. It's about connecting to what really matters and discarding what doesn't.

That is the gift of movement.

To know my sister was to have been moved by her, changed for the better. I know she wants us to keep moving... moving our breath through, moving our bodies while we are able, in whatever way we are able, in whatever way most brings us joy, moving in the direction of our dreams, moving toward effecting change, and moving closer to one another.

Catherine loved walks on the boardwalk, the wind on her face, the birds in the trees, the rustle of leaves on the ground. She loved tea roses and fresh spring flowers. She loved to move through the simple beauty of the world around her.

Take her wisdom along with you and be in love with movement and simple beauty and one another.

LITERACY MATTERS

Portions of profits from the sale of this book will be donated in Catherine's memory to the Children's Book Bank, providing literacy support to families in low-income neighbourhoods, community centres, health clinics, and schools across Toronto.

"CAM"
Catherine Anne McIntyre
October 17, 1963 to January 28, 2018

AFTERWORD

In the time since my sister's death, in observance of myself as I have waded through my process of grief, I have learned that profound inner peace and excruciating pain can coexist within me, that one does not cancel out the other, and that I can hold space for missing Catherine and wishing things were different while also continuing to live my own life, forge my own path, and bring my biggest dreams to fruition. If anything, losing her has given me even greater conviction in that regard.

I believe that the best way to cope with her light having been snuffed out too soon is to make my own light brighter.

Because I'm still alive. And as long as I am, I plan to *live*.

I hope the same is true for you.

with love, elemem

ACKNOWLEDGMENTS

I would like to thank Lenny Kravitz for unwittingly guiding me to Eleuthera where the real healing commenced and where the words began to flow in earnest—God bless the butterfly effect; Erin Cooper, for giving me professional publishing advice; Peter McAlpine, whose eyes were the first to see the poems that emerged in Eleuthera and offer feedback and ego-fortification; Daniel Wickie for introducing me to Peter; Barry Kuntz, who helped me find my voice; Valerie Dewar for being a lifelong and loving friend, ever-ready with words of encouragement; Britney Binkowski, who is the staunchest, most loyal and trusted comrade (and therapist) in life and who picked me up off the floor on the day of my sister's suicide and helped me dress, shower, eat, and find my feet again—Britney, I would be lost without you; Maribeth Collins, who loves me without reservation, makes me laugh until I cannot breathe, is a soul-sister to me and my most raucous cheerleader—Mari, you are my heart personified and I adore you endlessly; my brother-in-law, Ross Marancos, for loving Catherine unconditionally and for honouring her wishes even when it was hard; my sister, Susan, and her husband, Stuart, who held our family together during the worst time of our lives—Susan and Stuart, my gratitude overflows; my mother, Margie, for being a living model of unwavering love and total badassery—I'm proud to say I'm more like you, Mum, than I ever realized and being your daughter is truly my honour; and my son and ultimate Guru, Jazir, for whom my love is immeasurable and eternal, and my admiration unparalleled—I have no greater teacher in this life.

Posthumously I thank my sister Catherine McIntyre for challenging me, guiding me, forgiving me my faults, and for always wanting the best for me and aiming to provide it. My love for you is unending, in this and any realm. I miss you with my entire heart and soul. I pray you are running and biking and swimming through the stars somewhere overhead.. breathing.

say hello: elemem@insidestories.ca

13791012R00046

Made in the USA
Lexington, KY
03 November 2018